The Ghosts Of Belcourt Castle

HARLE H. TINNEY

EDITED BY TOM WINGETT

iUniverse, Inc.
New York   Bloomington

The Ghosts of Belcourt Castle

iUniverse books may be ordered through booksellers or by contacting:

iUniverse
1663 Liberty Drive
Bloomington, IN 47403
www.iuniverse.com
1-800-Authors (1-800-288-4677)

ISBN: 978-1-4401-9913-4 (sc)
ISBN: 978-1-4401-9911-0 (ebook)

Printed in the United States of America

iUniverse rev. date: 7/9/2010

Photography by Keith A. Henry and others

Contents

List of Photographs

Preface

The Royal Arts Foundation at Belcourt Castle proudly supports publishing *The Ghosts of Belcourt Castle*, by Mrs. Harle H. Tinney. Over the last fifteen years visitors to Belcourt Castle have shared their supernatural experiences while on our popular ghost tours, so we felt it was time to relate our own experiences in this volume.

The Tinney family had long encountered unexplained phenomena in their residence, but they refrained from sharing these stories until paranormal expert Virginia Smith's research confirmed evidence of Belcourt's ghosts. Many of these specters were found to be attached to antique in the museum's collection. As a visitor, Virginia first became aware of Belcourt's spirits, but later she was employed by the Royal Arts Foundation to present slide lectures on ghosts for the benefit of Belcourt's preservation. Her lecture focused not only on ghosts she had encountered in Newport, but also around the world. Because of their success, the Belcourt Ghost Lectures were expanded to include both a tour and a startling demonstration of paranormal energy in two chairs located in the ballroom of the castle.

During these tours Harle Tinney shared with visitors her own inexplicable experiences and those of other members of the Tinney family. Soon both Harle and Virginia began telling spellbound audiences eerie stories of hauntings at the castle, thereby introducing many of them to the museum's collection through this intriguing subject. This first volume contains Harle's stories through 2006, so we encourage you to visit Belcourt Castle to keep up with recent sightings. Dates and times of the "Ghosts of Belcourt" tours are listed at www.belcourtcastle.org. Your patronage will also help preserve the legacy of this remarkable historic structure through the non-profit Royal Arts Foundation

The Tinney family founded the Royal Arts Foundation in 1969 to preserve lost arts and historic creative processes. Their mission is to exhibit works of superb craftsmanship and artistry in the main rooms of Belcourt, an historic castle located on world-famous Bellevue Avenue in Newport, Rhode Island. Within this gem of both architectural and social history the Tinney family's collection of fine and decorative art pieces are displayed in spaces designed by the prominent American architect Richard Morris Hunt and the important Parisian decorator Jules Allard. The Board of Directors of the foundation makes every effort to protect the legacy of the Tinney family and their collection, which represents works from over 30 countries — with many pieces having formerly graced the interiors of some Newport's most fabled mansions.

Michael Kathrens, Author of "Newport Villas"

Foreword
by Virginia L. Smith

Belcourt Castle is full of ghosts. Indeed, it just may be the most haunted house in America. From dungeon to rafters, there is hardly a room in the mansion that can be said to be specter-free. I count fifteen of them: the man buried in concrete under the banquet hall; the poltergeist in the English library and elsewhere, who takes things and later returns them; the arm that points through the staircase; the lady in the ball gown in the second floor gallery; the pink lady, possibly Ruth Tinney, in Mrs. Belmont's bedroom; the British soldier, dressed in full regimentals; the Samurai warrior, whom I myself have seen; the white lady who walks through walls in the Grand Hall and gallery; the suit of armor that screams; the swishing battle axe in the weapons cabinet; the ghostly dancers in the French Gothic ballroom; the two spirits who haunt the medieval salt chairs; the ghost in the third floor maid's room; and above all, the mysterious monk statue.

Belcourt Castle, this magnificent house, is even more beautiful at twilight, when the lights are lowered and the phantoms emerge. But, beware! You must be brave to be in the house in the wee hours before dawn, for it is you and *whoever they are* who roam these halls.

Who hasn't dreamed of living in a castle? Which of us toads hasn't wanted to be king or queen for a day? You are about to read a fairy story about a twenty-year-old girl who, with her young husband, realized that dream. Harle Hanson married Donald

Harold Tinney, who, with his parents and a maiden great aunt, bought Belcourt and lovingly restored it and filled its stately halls with precious antiques. I wonder if they knew then that it was built over an early graveyard?

I think Harle and Donald Tinney may be the only persons who can truly rest in Belcourt Castle after the shadows lengthen and night sets in. At the end of this charming memoir of life in a haunted house, Harle claims she is still skeptical of ghosts. But they *are* here, of course.

Figure 2: Harle Tinney and Virginia Smith, a respected researcher and lecturer on the subject of ghosts. A "sensitive", one who is more able to detect the presence of spirits than is the average person, she has researched ghosts all over the globe. Her popular Ghost Lectures at Belcourt Castle are enjoyed by believers and skeptics alike. She is a member of the Ghost Club in England, the first organization in the world dedicated to exploring and understanding the spirit world.

Introduction

Belcourt is not haunted, despite the rumors. Yet on occasion some inexplicable apparitions have appeared to its owners, staff, and guests. The best explanation for those happenings, or at least the explanation most people prefer, is that there are ghosts in Belcourt Castle. If so, it is most likely that they came with the antiques, which are centuries older than the summer cottage Oliver Hazard Perry Belmont built in prestigious Newport, Rhode Island. It was designed in the Louis XIII style by famous architect Richard Morris Hunt, cost three million end-of-the-century dollars, and took three years to construct, from 1891 to 1894.

Figure 3: Belcourt Castle West Façade

For most of its first sixty years, the mansion afforded plenty of time for the spirits to cavort. Except for six weeks a year during that period, the mansion was uninhabited. That was not unusual; with few exceptions, the Newport mansions were considered "summer cottages."

Belmont married Alva Smith Vanderbilt, who had divorced the multi-millionaire railroad tycoon William K. Vanderbilt. They spent the next twelve summers at Belcourt, living a lavish lifestyle in a flurry of social events. After Oliver Belmont died in 1908, Alva made significant changes to Belcourt. She added the English library and the reception room that is now the chapel; she changed the staircase three times and gave the castle its first-ever kitchen. She died in France in 1933.

Belmonts owned the 60-room castle until 1940. In November 1956, Belcourt was purchased by Harold B. Tinney (55), his wife Ruth (50), their son Donald (23) and Ruth's aunt, Nellie Fuller (75).

Sensitives such as Virginia Smith have provided persuasive answers to many of the unexplained phenomena to which we paid little or no attention. She confided in me that, as a young girl, she had seen a ghost. It did not frighten her, but instead gave her the curiosity to do extensive research on the subject. Fascinated by the spirits she could sense among the historical artifacts at Belcourt Castle, she inquired about any unexplained visions we might have had. We attended one of her slide lectures on ghosts, and found it to be entertaining and informative. Her research and personal experiences, genuinely presented, dissolved my fear of being ridiculed for having seen The Monk apparition twice.

Now I relate my own experiences, and take the chance that some will understand.

Harle H. Tinney

Chapter I
Belcourt Is Not Haunted

Belcourt was abandoned from about 1940 until the mid 1950s, when a caretaker, Benny Collin, a Danish-born artist, took responsibility for keeping the vandals out.

Gaining illicit entry became a challenge. Twenty exterior entrances and more than 50 second story doors and windows were boarded up. Nonetheless, determined trespassers occasionally succeeded in getting in, and Benny could only repair the damage and replace the boards.

One particularly bad day, after boarding up yet another point of unlawful entry, Benny had an idea for catching the culprits, or for at least ensuring that they

Figure 4: Self-portrait of Benny Collin, artist, resident caretaker of Belcourt ca. 1948-1972

would never return. He bought a white sheet, a broom, and a flashlight. He moved his pallet bed from the cozy southeast corner studio to the cavernous third floor Musicians Balcony overlooking

Belcourt's French Gothic ballroom. From this central point, he could hear any activity in the eerie, echoing, empty halls.

After several nights of peace, Benny was awakened by the clump of footsteps on the grand stair. Intruders had found another way in! He threw his white sheet over himself and the broom, to which he had attached the flashlight. The barely five-foot tall Dane picked up a piece of chain he had gleaned from the beach after the 1954 hurricane, and waited until all the noises came from the ballroom. Then he lit the flashlight under the sheet, raised and lowered the broom, moaned, groaned, and rattled the chain. The startled intruders barely touched the stairs on their way out! Benny flew after them, his white sheet flapping in the wind. He chased them down the grand stair, across the marble floor toward the east basement, and through the ninety-foot tunnel.

Figure 5: Musicians Gallery with white sheet "ghost"

They went out as they had entered, through the tunnel door in the south courtyard. Down the dark street they ran. At Bailey's Beach, Benny, winded, gave up the chase.

Within a few days, the word had spread all over town: Belcourt was haunted. It worked! There were no more broken windows or damaged doors that season.

The Sequel: Years later, as I was giving a tour, I overheard a gentleman talking to his five-year-old grandson. "You know, son, if it weren't for you I never would have come back into this house."

Curious, I asked the man, "Why?"

"The last time I was in this house was over 35 years ago," he replied.

"Before the Tinneys bought the house?" I asked.

"Yeah," he said, "back when nobody was living here. Something chased me and some buddies of mine out of this house, and I swore that day that I would never come back here again. Wouldn't have, neither, if my grandson hadn't talked me into it."

That middle-aged grandfather had harbored the memory of Benny's sheet, broom and flashlight for 35 years!

Chapter II
Belcourt Becomes a Home

After Christmas in 1956, Belcourt groaned and creaked with a vibrant new life. Sixty years old, grand as it was, Belcourt had never felt the warmth of a family in residence.

Figure 6: The Tinney Family dines in Belcourt's
Versailles Dining Room

The Tinneys moved in with 17 van-loads of glorious furnishings. Over the first nine months that they lived in the castle, the active family added lights and heat, repaired doors and windows. The roof was fixed, the floors were polished, the dust and grime of years was washed away. The old "haunted house" became warm and hospitable.

At night, as the long-cold walls felt their first heat in decades, the mansion made noises. Loud bangs and booms resounded as the woodwork adjusted. Some might have been frightened by the eerie, nightly sounds, but not the Tinneys. The Tinneys did not believe in ghosts. And when Benny Collin shared the secret of his escapade with the sheet, they now understood the rumor that their home was haunted, and they laughed.

As each portion of the castle was furnished, more and more guests dropped in on weekends. One Saturday there were 50 friends and friends of friends. The guests persuaded the Tinneys to open Belcourt to the public on Saturday and Sunday afternoons. Gradually the museum became a popular attraction. Visitors praised its walls, its stained glass, and the collections inside. In 1958, the house was literally jumping with 1500 members and guests of President Dwight D. Eisenhower's press corps.

By 1959, the Tinneys had hired tour guides because they could no longer manage the influx of visitors on their own. And now that Belcourt had outgrown the cute "summer cottage" label, the Tinneys added to its name a word that means a large, imposing residence: "Castle."

Chapter III
The Bride

As a college student, I gave guided tours of Belcourt during my summer vacation. Donald Tinney inspired me with love and enthusiasm as he imparted his passion for the beautiful world of art. A talented musician, extraordinary artist, and tireless worker, Donald trained me as a guide. We fell in love, and were married in December, 1960. I moved into Belcourt Castle, eager to become a part of the Tinneys' magnificent world.

Figure 7: Donald and Harle Tinney's wedding picture
August 25, 1961

7

We had been married for about two weeks when, at around 4 a.m., something woke me. A man standing beside our bed seemed to be holding the canopy bedpost at my feet. I reasoned it must be Donald. But as I slid my hand a few inches under the sheet, I realized Donald was in bed. Fear crept over me. By the dim light of the streetlight outside the window, I could clearly see the form of a man silhouetted against the wall. As I debated whether or not I was dreaming, I began to fear that we might have a thief in the room. I imagined him with a gun or a knife, holding us hostage while the antiques and valuable pieces of the museum were being looted.

Hoping to wake Donald without letting the intruder know I was awake, I whispered, "Donald, there is someone standing beside the bed."

Donald softly answered "Go to sleep." The perfect answer for my robbery theory.

I lay as still as a corpse, eyes wide open, hardly breathing. The man turned slowly and walked about six feet past the bed—and right out through the wall. My sense of reality was shaken. "That is a *wall*," I thought. "There is no door there." For the next two hours, I lay perplexed, pondering my fate in an insane asylum. "I'm only nineteen," I mused.

On arising to start the day, I dared not say anything to Donald about my encounter with a specter. He'd think me crazy. I managed to remain silent until noon. When the entire family was enjoying lunch together, I finally related the strange incident of the night.

My mother-in-law began to laugh. "What did he look like?" she asked.

I replied, "I didn't see his face. He had something over his head—a hat or a hood. And he was dressed in a long coat that went all the way to the floor. It was a dark color."

Ruth looked at each of the three others at the table and asked, "Remember that night in "Seaverge"?" She explained to me that

"Seaverge" was the mansion on the ocean where the Tinneys lived in 1955 before they bought Belcourt.

Figure 8: The Tinney Family in "Seaverge" Library in 1956
Photo by Jerry Taylor

"One night after dinner, the four of us—Harold, Donald, Aunt Nellie, and I, the only people at home that evening—were sitting in our *petit salon*. It had a fireplace at one end of the room and a door to the 90-foot-long main hall at the other. We all saw a man walk by that door.

"We immediately jumped up to accost the intruder. Reaching the hall within seconds, we found no trace of a person. We had heard no sounds: no doors opening or closing, no windows being raised, no footsteps on the polished marble. We didn't want to go to bed with an intruder in the house, so we searched it, all 43 rooms, attic to basement. We looked under servants' beds, in closets and coal bins, to no avail. Nevertheless, we all agreed, before retiring two hours later, that we *had* seen a man with a long brown coat and a hat that covered his face."

The family concurred as she added, "I haven't thought of that in years."

The word "ghost" never came up in the conversation during that lunch.

If the apparition I had seen during the night was the same as the one Ruth described, and today I am certain it was, then it must have come to Belcourt with the Tinneys—or rather, with some of the furniture and works of art they brought to the castle. Eventually, we would discover how that could have happened.

For now, it was enough that we seemed to agree that it meant no harm. And without realizing how appropriate the name would prove to be, we nicknamed our apparition "The Monk."

The Sequel 2009: In 2008, I renovated the second floor of the west wing, beginning with the bedroom where I slept on my wedding night in 1960. Under the supervision of my architect, Richard R. Long, carpenters moved a partition to create a kitchen where there had been a bathroom. Later, I decided to add a door between the reception area and the conference room. When the carpenter cut an opening in the wall for the doorway, he discovered that in 1894 there had been a door there. Though the new door was a few inches offset from the original door's location, I felt happy about the change as a historical restoration.

Early in 2009, I was showing a friend the completed renovations. Pensively I reminisced that the room we were standing in had been the bedroom I moved into nearly fifty years before. I recounted the night I had seen my first ghost, who had walked out through the wall. I pointed toward that wall. After being walled in for more than sixty years, the door was there once more!

Chapter IV
The Monk

The Tinney family bought a stained glass studio in Providence, Rhode Island, in early 1961. Monday through Friday, except for July and August, Harold, Ruth, Donald, and I commuted together between Belcourt and the studio.

One morning, as was our custom, Donald and I secured the first floor of Belcourt to be certain that all was in order before we left. Similarly, Ruth and Harold inspected the second floor. Don and I were waiting at the foot of the stairs for Ruth and Harold to walk to the automobile with us. Normally we all finished at about the same time. But this day was different.

After a few minutes of waiting, Donald and I saw what we assumed was Harold, wearing his winter coat and hat, walk across the end of the Grand Hall in front of the green glass. Since we did not see him

Figure 9: The monk appears in the Grand Hall in front of the Ladies' Room. Photo enhanced by Keith Henry

11

coming toward us after that, we assumed he had gone into the ladies room to double-check the water. That room is very small, and would take only a few seconds to inspect. But he was in there a *long* time.

Waiting for Harold to reappear and for Ruth to come down the grand stair, Donald and I were engrossed in conversation. Don was always teaching me about the beautiful antiques and their history, the sagas of their acquisition, and the people who had owned them. Every piece had a story.

Suddenly, Aunt Nellie appeared on the staircase landing; "They've been waiting for you in the car for fifteen minutes." Her voice was strident, and she seemed a bit annoyed.

"No, Aunt Nellie," said Don. "Mom is in the car, but Dad is in the ladies' room."

Aunt Nellie replied positively, "They are *both* in the car."

Don and I looked at each other. "Then, who's that in the ladies room?"

Donald rushed to the ladies room as I went out to the car, where Ruth and Harold were indeed waiting. Now in a panic, I told them about the man in the ladies room, and said that Don would need help. Without any hesitation, they both jumped out of the car and hurried to the Grand Hall.

Don, looking puzzled, was standing alone in the middle of the hall. "There was nobody there," he said.

Pondering how a person could have escaped our notice when leaving that room, we decided to search the whole building before we left. We were not eager to leave our elderly Aunt Nellie alone with a trespasser or thief.

Then Harold Tinney thought better of the idea, and inquired simply, "Did you *hear* anything?"

"No," we agreed.

With that, Harold opened the ladies room door, and in so doing, reminded us of its customary loud creak, a noise to which we were so accustomed that we had not given it a thought. No,

12

we *hadn't* heard anything, but as Harold was demonstrating, we should have.

Without telling Aunt Nellie about our experience, we left her alone with The Monk.

Chapter V
The Cassone

Another experience on our daily commute, driving home to Newport from Providence, gives rise to the theory that spirits sometimes work by making mental suggestions: no words, no visions, and no absolutes.

One night, Donald inexplicably asked, "Let's not take the highway. Can we go the old way?" Behind the wheel, Mom was tired after twelve hours of work, but she trusted Donald's intuition.

It was after six in the evening, and the stop-and-go traffic allowed us time to observe the surroundings. Though familiar in many ways, the old road seemed changed, transformed by the new buildings that dotted the once tranquil countryside.

We stopped at a red light, and Don noticed a sign, "Antiques," diagonally across the intersection. "Let's stop here." he said.

"Why not?" we agreed.

"We can telephone Aunt Nellie and tell her that we'll be home later than usual, so she won't worry," said Ruth.

Pulling up in front of the store, we saw only one other car in front. A very dim light shone in the shop, but the OPEN sign was hanging on the door. A bell announced our arrival as we entered. There was very little light, so we moved slowly and cautiously through the shop. It was chock-full of furniture and bric-a-brac.

Breaking an eerie silence, a distant voice startled us. "There is a medium in the room."

We could see no one. Then a crack of light back-lit a short figure as she opened a door from the back room. Dressed in black slacks and a black sweater, the mature woman emerged and turned on light switches until the place was fully illuminated.

She stared at the four of us, and then pointed at Donald. "You are the medium."

This was rather strange, and I think we all felt uncomfortable. The eerie feeling slowly passed, however, once the woman introduced herself and began to make pleasant small talk. She had been working after hours, she told us, repairing some lampshades, and did not expect to have any customers after dark.

It took some time to go through the shop. There were so many things, mostly Victorian. Don, exploring on his own, ferreted out a very early cassone, buried under some rugs and tapestries covered with small antique pieces. We guessed that the large and elaborately carved piece had been there a very long time, since it was way in the back of the shop. After inquiring about several of the more showy pieces of furniture, Don asked about the chest.

"It came from a big Newport mansion," the woman said. It was a long time ago; she could not recall which mansion.

After some discussion, Don convinced us that we must own that antique Italian chest. It was hundreds of years old, probably older than anything else in the shop.

We came to terms and bought the cassone. Extricating it from the store without damaging other merchandise took care and skill. Don and Harold loaded it like a casket into the back of the old 1955 Ford station wagon. While I sat in the front seat with Dad and Mom, Don had to sit cross-legged beside the chest for the rest of the trip.

In the daylight, we unloaded the beautifully carved piece. Our preliminary research told us that the low, walnut *cassone*, likely used as a bridal or dower chest, had been created about 1390 A.D.

Figure 10: Italian walnut cassone ca. 1390

On the back, written in faint pencil, we could distinguish the letters "OHP Belmont." Whatever guided us through that bizarre evening had seen to it that we brought the piece "home."

Years later, a local photographer gave us a picture from 1914 of that very chest in Belcourt's first floor Grand Hall—further proof that this medieval antique now was, and still is, where it should be.

Chapter VI
Strange Noises

From about 1966 to 1976, we lived in Belcourt's main wing, which is the museum. Harold and Ruth slept in the Louis XV bedroom, formerly that of Alva Belmont, while Donald and I slept in Oliver Belmont's master bedroom.

Figure 11: Belcourt's Medieval style Master Bedroom.
Photo by Residential Properties

The summers were wonderful, but in winter the rooms often were chilly, especially when strong winds blew through small gaps in the French doors.

Night noises were common. With windows open, sounds drifted in from miles away over the ocean. The Brenton Reef lightship sounded a forlorn "whoo grump" as fog rolled in. The lightship was later replaced by a "Texas Tower" lighthouse that had a piercing siren. Fog meant a noisy night. Nonetheless, we slept peacefully most nights after a long day's work.

On one occasion, however, a sense of fear enveloped our bedroom shortly after midnight. We heard strange noises emanating from the ballroom. There were people moving around, echoing music playing, and ball gowns swishing on the oak floor. This latter sound was particularly puzzling, as we now had large rugs covering most of the floor. Our huge coal black cat, "Graf Loki von Schwartz", who slept on our bed, jumped down and put his nose to the door. His tail bristled and his back arched like the classical Halloween cat. A cold draft chilled the air, and even the down comforter and the velvet spread were not enough to warm us.

Neither of us felt like opening the ballroom door, which had no lock at the time. Comfort and security overcame curiosity for me, but Don got up to investigate. The huge oak door creaked as he opened it slowly. The noises ceased. All was silent and calm. He found no evidence of people having come into the house, and everything was just as it had been the day before.

We calmed our nerves by recalling that several times birds or bats had flown around in the ballroom, and sometimes in the bedroom, especially in late summer when we had left windows open. The cat had reacted to those, of course, but had not displayed fear. It was not a perfect explanation, but it was reasonable. And sometimes reasonable explanations are very comforting.

Chapter VII
Conversation with a Ghost

Another night, as we slept in the master bedroom, Donald began a conversation with an unseen visitor. As though I was listening to one side of a telephone conversation, I heard him say, "Yes, Tom." "Of course, Tom." "I will." "Nan will be alright. I'll take care of her." The episode mystified me, but I did not try to interfere with the conversation in his dream.

When we got up around seven, the phone rang. It was a distraught Nan Wilson, our friend, neighbor, and a Belcourt Castle tour guide. Her husband, Tom, had passed away during the night, and she would not be coming to work for a few days.

Don kept his promise to Tom, made that night in his audible "dream," as Nan grew older. She conducted tours well into her late seventies. After an illness forced her to retire, we visited her often and kept in touch until she joined Tom some ten years later.

Chapter VIII
The Monk Speaks

New, young tour guides arrived every season. A particularly sensitive college girl, a history buff, came downstairs with her tour one day and reported that somebody in the ballroom had told her to "Get out." There were only four visitors on her tour, all of them pleasant, so she knew that none of them had uttered the words. "It wasn't a person. It came from a statue." she said.

Though we believed her story in one sense, logic argued that she probably had overheard part of a distant conversation, perhaps a neighbor whose voice had carried across the street on that particular day. We also considered that the words she had heard were in English, yet the statue is German. We therefore felt the words were more likely sensed than actually heard.

That tour guide "heard" the same thing several times after that, and became increasingly uncomfortable in the ballroom.

Figure 12: French Gothic Ballroom, Belcourt's most haunted room

Though she completed the season, she expressed her belief that something in the house did not like her, and she would seek other employment the next summer.

Chapter IX
The Monk Walks Again

In my opinion, the funniest ghost story happened when Kurt, the teenage boyfriend of a tour guide, came to pick up his girlfriend.

It was an extremely hot day in August, and a group of senior citizens had just enjoyed Belcourt's elegant afternoon tea. About 15 minutes after they had boarded their bus and left, while we were cleaning up, Kurt hobbled up to the door on crutches.

He asked Ruth Tinney, "Can Sue go home a little early?"

Ruth observed his pale and uncomfortable condition. She indicated a plush chair in the solarium where he could sit and wait. "You have just walked over 200 feet! Sit and rest for 15 minutes. We'll be finished by then, and Sue can leave."

As he sat near the door to the Grand Hall and solarium, he called out in a loud voice, "Hey! Go stop the bus. They left someone." The young tour guides scurried outside in a vain attempt to catch the bus, while Ruth and I queried Kurt about *who* had missed the bus.

"It was an old guy," Kurt said. "He walked out of the chapel and down that way and ... and I guess I didn't see where he went after that. Maybe through that door." Kurt pointed toward the door of the ladies room.

Hearing that, I went to find the gentleman, while Ruth started planning a course of action to reunite him with the group, now well on its way to Cape Cod. Surmising that I would find the man in the Grand Hall, I was puzzled when I saw nobody.

After a quick run through the adjoining rooms, glancing behind doors and looking in likely hiding spots, I guessed that Kurt had been right, and the lost tourist must be in the ladies room. The door was closed. I listened for a moment. Hearing nothing, I gently knocked on the door. There was no reply. I knocked louder. "Sir, are you alright?" With visions of him passed out on the floor, perhaps from the heat, I opened the door a crack. The room was empty.

Again I looked through the chapel and the banquet hall, finally making my way back to Kurt. "I can't find him. What did he look like?" I asked.

"Well, he was an old guy, like I said. He had on a long coat—brown. And he was wearing a hat, kind of an odd looking hat. I didn't see his face, though."

All of a sudden, I knew that he had seen The Monk. "You saw the ghost," I said. I told him a little about our past experiences in the same area of the Grand Hall.

That was all Kurt needed to hear. He picked up his crutches and headed for the exit. Over his shoulder he cried, "Tell Sue I'll wait for her in the car!"

That was the last we saw of him. Sue complained that, after that day, when Kurt came to pick her up, come rain or shine he would make her walk the 600 feet from the house out to Bellevue Avenue. He would not even drive onto the property.

These strange incidents have no easy explanation. The Tinney family never made any attempt to discover the source of the phenomena. That was not a priority.

Chapter X
The Disbelievers

In 1966, the Tinney family undertook a project to build a full-scale replica of an 18th century Portuguese coronation coach. Donald designed the wrought iron frame of the coach, which we would then overlay with carved wood. Ruth Tinney's brother Glenn, our "Uncle Glenn," just retired from a job he had held for 40 years, agreed to help us for a year. He was the metal worker in the family, and his skills and resources for welding were invaluable. He taught Donald how to use the arc welder and oxy-acetylene torch, and when to use each.

We had hardly begun when, on the second Friday of his stay, Uncle Glenn announced at the breakfast table that he was going home. "But, Glenn, we need you," said Ruth. "Why must you leave?"

He replied politely, "I can't get any sleep in this house."

"Is the mattress uncomfortable? We'll get you a new one today; that is not a problem," said Ruth, as she tried to make him feel more at home.

"The mattress is fine," Glenn replied.

"Is it the food? Our schedule? Why can't you stay?" Ruth inquired.

"If I tell you, you won't believe me," Glenn said.

But eventually, we coaxed him into telling this story:

"Last Tuesday night, I awoke because I was cold. All the bedcovers were in a heap on the floor. In all my life, I have not tossed and turned enough to throw off the covers like that. It occurred to me that maybe one of you folks was playing a practical joke on me. I picked up the covers, tucked the blankets in all around, and crawled in from the top. Comfortable again, I fell asleep. Shortly I was awakened again, and found the covers on the floor. That happened three times on Tuesday night, and again three times on Wednesday night. And last night, after I had another tug of war with the guy pulling down the covers, a guy I couldn't see, I said, 'Enough! I'm going home.' I'm sorry, but you can't change my mind. I will not spend another night in this house."

What could we say? Nothing like that had happened before.

Uncle Glenn drove home in his new Mustang convertible. In his hometown library, he read every book he could find that might offer some explanation for his experience with the unseen person pulling off his bed covers.

Three months later, Uncle Glenn returned, armed with a theory that Belcourt was full of electromagnetic energy. He had discovered that an underground stream moves the length of the structure about 12 feet below the surface. "Those loose electrons pulled the covers off my bed," he reasoned.

Figure 13: Exterior of Belcourt with sculpture from Vernon Court

The Westerly granite in Belcourt's corners, window sills, keystones, cornices, and door surrounds also has a very strong energy field, which Glenn demonstrated with a divining rod. Put into drinking water, high energy stones are said to pass on their energy. So while Glenn was here, we drank granite water.

Chapter XI
The Mysterious Hand

Harold Tinney, born in 1901, always pooh-poohed the ghost stories that Donald and I told. Despite having seen The Monk in Seaverge, he tended to be quite skeptical— until early one evening in late summer.

We had scheduled a bus tour to arrive after normal hours. About ten minutes before the bus was due, Harold went into the museum to turn on the lights. As he stepped out of the apartment door onto the staircase landing, he turned back and began shouting. "Ruth, Donny, Harle. Come quick, come quick!" We thought that maybe the house was afire.

We found him standing on the landing, looking bewildered, and muttering, "It's gone. There was a hand, right over there." He pointed to the tall newel post which supports the third floor balcony. "There was a hand, without a body. It was pointing over there, toward the painting of picture of Mary Magdalene on staircase.

Figure 14: Painting of Mary Magdalene, enhanced by Keith Henry

It was a story that was hard to believe, yet we believed it, all the same. Harold described details, and he was noticeably shaken.

Suddenly we remembered the bus tour. The four of us scurried to turn on lights and open doors. Our plan was that Ruth Tinney would take half the group, while I was to guide the other half. Donald and Harold would open and close the outside gates and provide security.

The guests arrived. We divided the group so that the tours would be one room apart. The first group ascended the grand stair, reaching the top as the second group arrived at the foot of the stairs.

Figure 15: Francis I Grand Stair

All of a sudden, the painting of Mary Magdalene, in its heavy, gilded baroque frame, fell with a loud crash, smashing the frame to bits in the middle of the staircase.

The tour upstairs went on, but the second tour was held back until Donald and Harold cleared the stairs of the painting and what remained of its frame.

To this day, we are mystified. Had the painting fallen half a minute sooner or later, one of the tours would have been passing the exact spot where the painting fell, and undoubtedly one or more of the guests would have been injured.

Was the mysterious hand a warning that something was awry? Or did the hand itself cut the cable that fastened the painting to the woodwork ten feet above the stairs? We all observed that the cable was not frayed, stretched, or pulled apart. It appeared to have been cut, as if with wire cutters, near the ceiling. That no one was hurt was a blessing, one of many that have saved the Tinney family much grief.

Today there is a large gilded mirror where the painting hung on the stair. Restored, the Guido Reni *Mary Magdalene* hung for years in the English Library.

Chapter XII
The Pope

Belcourt Castle *was* blessed—literally. On the day the Tinneys purchased the castle, Cistercian monks at the Spencer Abbey in Massachusetts were directing their prayers toward Belcourt. One of the monks, son of a socially prominent family and an antique lover and designer, had become a close friend and a supporter of the Belcourt Castle adventure. He nicknamed the Tinney's home "The Monastery in Newport." When the monks received donations of beautiful paintings and furniture that were inappropriate or unneeded, they often traded them for art work and furniture that the Tinneys created to the monastery's specifications.

Brother B, in an effort to help the Tinneys fund their fledgling museum, introduced the family to a wealthy businesswoman who had collected many magnificent museum-quality treasures on her world tour after she sold her multi-million-dollar business. Clara loved the Catholic Church because "they put on the best show." But the Church wanted little of her secular collections, though it always was pleased with her large monetary donations.

Among her treasures was a sterling silver Renaissance reliquary. She called it her "Old Priest." The triple crown over the beautifully sculptured bust indicated it was a priceless object. It had an inscription, but because the silver was tarnished nearly black, it was barely discernible, and not at all legible.

Clara, then more than eighty years old, was diagnosed with liver cancer. She adored Donald, and one afternoon when we were visiting her at her home in Norwood, Massachusetts, she impulsively offered him her "Old Priest." "It must go to a church or a museum. I like you people. You'll take care of it." And so the silver bust began its journey to Belcourt Castle.

We saw something bizarre on the way home from Norwood that afternoon. There were six of us in the car: four Tinneys, Benny Collin, and the "Old Priest." Benny, sitting in the front seat, remarked about the glorious sky and the unusual cloud formations. "Look up there," he said. "It looks like a perfect cross."

Benny was right. A gray cloud in the shape of a cross hung in the sunset sky among the pink, purple, and gold-tinged cumulus clouds. We stared at the cloud, and noticed that it did not dissipate. It seemed to stay in front of us all the way, even though the road often changed direction on our southward journey. We watched the sunset, and remarked again and again that the mysterious cloud was still there.

As we pulled up to the Ledge Road door of Belcourt about an hour later, daylight was nearly gone. Yet our dark cross in the clouds was still visible in the western sky.

Donald carried the fourteen-pound silver bust into the house. Aunt Nellie had dinner ready, so we dined.

After dinner, Donald began to polish the reliquary. First, he removed the hand-made bolts holding the brooch, a cast silver frame surrounding a clear glass oval. The glass was so dirty that you couldn't see anything inside. Once he had removed the glass, Donald found an old piece of paper, neatly folded, with writing that had faded so badly over the centuries that it was practically unreadable. The only words we could read without subjecting the paper to a more sophisticated analysis were "St. Sylvester."

Lying in the bottom of the frame, where it had fallen when the silk thread that been used to display it had rotted away, was a pea-sized fragment of what appeared to be bone. We had not expected to find a relic, because it was customary that when a piece such as this bust left the church, any "holy part" was removed and buried. But now we had to consider the possibility that we had found a relic.

Figure 16: Cabinet containing the silver reliquary of Pope St. Sylvester I. Photo 1978 by Yankee Colour

As Donald polished the pedestal, which contained the inscription, we could read "Sancta Sylvester, Papa Cofessor [sic]." It began to appear that Clara's priest was actually a pope.

Mom and I researched Sylvester I in the encyclopedia, and confirmed our suspicions. We discovered that he had been the pope between 313 and 335 A.D. Reading further, we learned that he had presided over the Nicene council at the time the Nicene Creed was composed, and that he had baptized Constantine shortly before the emperor's death. This was the bust of no ordinary pope!

All of a sudden, a sense of awe permeated the room as we connected our vision of the gray cross in the sky with the momentous conversion of Constantine. Legend has it that in 312 A.D., before the battle that would establish his rule over the entire western Roman empire, the pagan emperor saw a cross in the sky with the inscription "IN HOC SIGNO VINCES" (in this sign, conquer). The following year, Constantine became the first Christian emperor.

The relic could be genuine. Respecting its possible sanctity, we returned it and the folded paper so they could be seen through the glass, now cleaned and polished. We were many times blessed in the years that followed. *Ghosts never appeared during the years that the holy reliquary resided in the family chapel*

In the wee hours of a Sunday in the summer of 1983, the morning after 2,000 guests had attended the Tall Ships Ball at Belcourt, thieves came in through a door we never used. They broke the locked cabinet containing the reliquary, and stole the bust of the pope, along with countless other silver pieces.

Although many of the stolen items were found by police after they received an anonymous tip, the reliquary bust was not among them.

Chapter XIII
The Believers

In the early years, the ghosts we experienced were like exemplary Victorian children: seen, but not heard. Therefore, I felt there must be another explanation for the feral screams I heard one evening in the ballroom.

In late March of 1994, the castle was still closed for the winter. Early one evening, I needed to bring something from the museum into the private apartments. I came out onto the staircase landing through the door that connects the wings.

From the landing, I saw that the six spotlights were illuminating the 13th century windows in the Gothic ballroom. Seeing no reason for burning the electricity when the museum was closed, I turned off the switches, which were located on the far side of the ballroom.

Figure 17: Thirteenth Century stained glass
in the French Gothic Ballroom

Crossing back in the dark, I heard a terrifying scream that seemed to come from someone, or something, nearly beside me. Stunned and scared, I stopped in my tracks. Then, regaining my composure, I theorized that the third floor resident was playing a joke, trying to frighten me.

"You really scared me. That's not funny," I uttered, as I looked up toward the Musicians Balcony. When no sound came from the balcony, not a word or a giggle, my heart started pounding. Trying to remain calm, I resumed my mission until I glanced backward. The lights I had just turned off were on again. Determined to put them out, I returned to the ballroom.

The second scream was worse than the first!

Nonetheless, I switched the lights off again, making certain that they clicked audibly.

A third scream pierced the silence with debilitating effect. I forgot what I had gone into the museum to retrieve. I ran back into the private quarters and picked up the office telephone to call the man on the third floor and berate him for scaring me. His roommate answered and assured me that they were not involved. I believed him.

Donald and I decided to get our dogs to sniff out the source of the horrendous, animal-like noises. He put leashes on Samson and Delilah, our Rottweilers, in the south wing, while the two dogs from the third floor, Shelby and Gretchen, were let loose. Neither would enter the ballroom, and Don could not pull Samson and Delilah past the landing on the stairs. Seeing the animals react so strangely, Don simply said, "Don't worry, it's just the ghost."

Virginia Smith, a recognized expert and lecturer on the subject of ghosts, has explained that the Italian armor, a 16th century battle suit, has an angry spirit. She heard his loud, feral growl many times when she took tours into the ballroom. She refused to go into that room alone at night.

Figure 18: Italian battle armor ca. 1450

Rarely frightened by ghosts, having spent her life seeking them in her world travels, Miss Smith feels this spirit is different. Her explanation is based on the fact that there had been extensive damage to the helmet, likely caused by a blow from a pointed weapon. (Donald repaired the large hole when he acquired the rare suit.)

Miss Smith senses that the knight died an agonizing death while wearing that suit in battle. A serious head wound, which the condition of the helmet suggested its wearer had received, may have rendered him unconscious, resulting in his being left for dead by his comrades. He could have suffered interminable and unimaginable pain before he died.

After we made mention of frightening noises in the ballroom, several people, including the piano tuner, reported hearing loud, terrifying screams there.

A Girl Scout troop visited the castle early one April. A twelve-year-old scout screamed as she heard sounds coming from the armor and saw the armor raise its right arm. Several of the other girls corroborated the story, as did the guide.

Although the knight is most likely to act up in late March or early April (could that have been the time of year when the knight died in battle?) one group of guests reported hearing the loud, snarling scream while they stood near the armor in July, 2004.

Chapter XIV
Discovering the Monk

In the early 1990s, Virginia Smith did some research on our German woodcarving of a monk. She wanted to learn whether the monk could be placed in a particular sect or age. The unusual helmet and the carved, wooded habit are similar to others found in early tapestries and paintings. She was also curious about something written on the book the monk holds, something undecipherable. Is it just a design invented by the artist? Or could it be a mystic language understood only in the spirit world? Although these are questions that Virginia has yet to answer, she continues to believe they are significant.

During the same period when Virginia was researching the statue, a guide who was conducting a tour of the castle was suddenly interrupted in the Grand Hall by a guest who declared, in a loud, high-pitched voice, "That statue told me it wants to be in the chapel!" The words came from a short, blond woman who was standing in front of the monk. Her outburst startled the guests and stymied the guide, leaving him wondering what to do with the "nut" on his tour. Begging forgiveness for the interruption, the woman asked for time after the tour to explain. When she tried to do so, however, she had to admit that she couldn't explain; she had no idea why the statue had spoken to her. She knew only that it had.

Dorothie Maksym, Doctor of Theology and a medium, provided a theory connecting the statue with the strange figure which frequently appears wearing a long brown coat, or robe, and a hat that conceals his face. She told us that the realistically carved statue, likely pre-seventeenth century, is imbued with energy. At certain times, one might see this energy, this spirit, by looking beyond the statue at a plain surface. If there is an aura—sometimes small, sometimes wide—around the statue, the spirit is strong. Most of the time, however, the aura is not there: The spirit of the monk is not home.

Figure 19: Seventeenth Century German woodcarving of a monk

On one occasion when she was standing near the statue, Dr. Maksym heard a voice speak to her. No one else heard it, but Dr. Maksym was unequivocal about it. She said the voice was so clear that it was almost as if she was having a conversation with whomever, or whatever, was speaking to her.

Conjecturing that Dr. Maksym's impromptu communication had been not with the statue, but with its spirit—The Monk—the family tried to recall every instance when the dark, robe-clad figure had been seen traversing slowly across a room. We concluded that, amazingly, the statue was always nearby.

At "Seaverge," the statue had been placed on a *cassone* in the hall opposite the door to the petit salon, the room where Ruth Tinney saw The Monk. When I watched the robed figure pass through our bedroom wall, the statue was on a table just twenty feet away. The statue was in the center of the ballroom when our tour guide heard "Get out." And for more than twenty years, the statue stood on an Italian chest near the ladies room door in the Grand Hall, both places where The Monk was frequently seen.

The Monk is a restless spirit. Several persons who understand ghosts—sensitives or mediums—have tried to determine why that is so. So far, there has been no definitive answer. But I have heard one very interesting hypothesis. In the mid 1990s, during a large dinner party in the castle's Italian banquet hall, guests sitting at a table located near the entrance to the chapel told us an intriguing story.

Although the party was buzzing with music and light-hearted conversation, and despite the efforts of some to redirect the conversation to a more festive subject, these guests had carried on a serious discussion about the supernatural. This had eventually led to the subject of Nazism. One educated woman recalled learning about a Renaissance-period monk whose writings, she told the group, had formed the basis for Hitler's philosophy of ethnic purity.

After the dinner, that guest spoke with me. She told me she had been surprised to hear herself talking about spirits in general, and about that ancient monk in particular. She had never mentioned him before, she said; indeed, she hadn't thought about him in years. Aware that she had been sitting very close to the statue, I confided to her that she may have been influenced by The Monk.

Hearing that, the guest suggested the possibility that the monk ("her" monk, but perhaps also ours?) may have been attempting to communicate through her. Distraught by the degree to which his treatise had been misinterpreted and used with such horrific results in the twentieth century, perhaps he hoped to find peace by having her speak for him.

Sometime after we moved the statue of the monk into the family chapel, one visitor left a tour to go to the ladies' room in the Grand Hall. Passing through the chapel, she noticed a priest preparing the altar.

When she passed the front desk on her way back to her tour, she stopped to inquire about services held in the chapel. "Is there a service today?" she asked.

The desk attendant was not aware of any service scheduled, and wondered why the woman had asked.

"I saw a priest preparing the altar," she said sincerely.

Figure 20: Belcourt's Family Chapel

Leaving her desk to go find out what the priest was doing, the attendant looked into the chapel. Seeing no one there, nor in the banquet hall, she asked, "What did he look like?"

Our guest described a man she had assumed to be a priest, wearing a long brown robe and a hood. His back was toward her, so she had not seen his face.

Hesitantly, the attendant suggested that she had seen the famous Belcourt Monk—that is, she explained, a ghost. The lady, visibly disturbed, left the castle and did not complete the tour.

Chapter XV
The Secret Door

The portrait photographer at the Coast Guard Academy graduation gala in March, 2001, was on his last trip from the music room. It was two o'clock in the morning, and he was talking his camera equipment downstairs. We met at the foot of the grand staircase. At the beginning of the evening, I had tried to impress on him that he was responsible for the safety of the artwork in the music room, and therefore he should not allow anyone to go behind the rope.

"How did everything go?" I asked.

"Everything was fine," he said, "until a few minutes ago, when a man walked across the room behind the rope. He went out through the door to the left of the fireplace." He paused, and then added, "Uh, there is a door there, isn't there?"

Figure 21: Francis I Music Room

"There is a secret door there," I replied, "but it hasn't been opened in years. In fact, a painting hangs over part of it, and there is furniture in front of it." I asked what the man looked like.

"He was dressed completely in dark clothes, including a hat and a long coat."

When I heard his description, I surmised that the photographer had seen The Monk. But I thought this was somewhat unusual, because The Monk normally manifested itself near the statue.

Then I remembered that the statue now was in the chapel, which meant it was directly below where the figure had appeared. I told the photographer about our Monk, and said that it probably was what he saw. After a little discussion, the skeptical photographer left the castle. The following year, he sent an assistant to photograph the graduation ball.

Chapter XVI
Other Ghosts

Two spirits in our castle never appear. They silently inhabit the pair of Gothic throne chairs in the ballroom.

In medieval times, a high-back arm chair, a throne chair, was reserved for the king or the lord of the manor. All others sat on backless benches. The chair was constructed so that the monarch could store valuables such as precious salt and spices in a secret chest below the hinged seat, which is why these chairs are sometimes referred to as "salt chairs." Virginia Smith calls them that.

One day when she was visiting the castle, Virginia demonstrated a peculiarity of our dark oak French throne chair.

Figure 22: Virginia Smith demonstrates energy left behind in the French salt chair

Standing perfectly still beside the chair, eyes closed, she lowered her hand ever so slowly from the top of the back of the chair down toward the seat until she had reached the bottom. Then she asked Don and me to do the same thing. We did.

The feeling was indescribable, and very mysterious. Nevertheless, I tried to dismiss it. After all, it was just a chair—an authentic and rare 14th century museum exhibit, to be sure, but just a chair, nothing more.

Then Virginia moved to the English linen-fold paneled chair beside it, and asked us to perform the same maneuver. This time I felt something different. Donald apparently did too, for his reaction was noticeably stronger than it had been with the first chair. Then he walked away, slowly rubbing his hand. What was this? "Energy left behind," was Virginia's simple answer.

On subsequent demonstrations with guests who came to hear Virginia Smith's Ghost Lecture, I saw many guests have pronounced reactions to those chairs. The most astounding incident happened on a summer Thursday several years ago.

A large group of ghost enthusiasts watched Virginia demonstrate her method of detecting whether the "French lady" was sitting in the chair at that moment. A female volunteer from the assemblage followed Virginia's example. She held her hand above the chair, palm down, and slowly began to lower it. When her hand was about head-level in the chair, she suddenly stopped. Her face became contorted, her eyes rolled back, and she seemed to be in trouble. Virginia softly asked her to continue lowering her hand. "I can't," the woman replied in a painfully unsteady voice. "Something is holding my hand."

I watched Virginia try to gently coax the woman away from the chair, away from whatever was obstructing her hand. Her words had no effect; the woman was frozen in place. Virginia told me later, "When I looked at her face, everything was popping all over it. She was in seizure. I had to do something, and fast."

What Virginia did was slash back and forth aggressively between the woman's hand and the seat of the chair. As she did that, a white, fiery ball, as bright as a magnesium flash, virtually exploded into existence. It appeared to start from the seat of the chair, near Virginia's hand, then traveled up and over the group, trailing a puff of acrid smoke. The smell lingered, as if something electrical was burning. But there was nothing electrical, not even an outlet, within twenty feet of that chair.

As the woman was still held captive by the chair, Virginia dragged her away to release her. Almost instantly the woman returned to her normal appearance.

Virginia seemed dazed. Experiencing extreme stomach pain, she rushed down the grand stairway ahead of the guests to take refuge in private. It was obvious that the tour was over. I waited upstairs until all the guests had descended the stairs.

"Virginia is in the ladies room," one of my staff informed me.

From outside the door, I called to her, "Are you alright?"

She was not. She said she was on the floor, unable to get up. With her were two of the tour guests who, fortuitously, happened to be paramedics. "Leave me. I'll be OK. Just give me some time." She asked one of the paramedics for a drink of cognac. He relayed the request, but the only thing handy was some wine. Virginia settled for that.

After about an hour, she arose on her own, left the ladies room, and walked unsteadily to a chair. Then she asked, "Is the woman alright? I am worried about her."

I replied, "The woman seemed fine, Virginia. In fact, she was more concerned about your welfare than about what had happened to her. She was grateful for the quick thinking you showed. The whole group was anxious to stay to see if you were going to be OK. What in the world happened?"

"I was zapped," she said in a hushed voice. "I knew what the consequences could be, but I did it anyway. I took the whole jolt."

After that incident, we had not the slightest doubt that the French chair in the ballroom contains some entity with great power which can distress a person who invades its space. I had never before witnessed anything that dramatic involving the spirit world, and even today I am uneasy just thinking about it.

Chapter XVI
Christmas Party Apparition

A corporate Christmas party for several hundred guests was held on December 17, 1996. It was, by coincidence, the eve of the first anniversary of Ruth Tinney's death. To accommodate that many guests, Mrs. Belmont's bedroom became a waiting area for the second floor ladies room, originally Mrs. Belmont's bathroom.

Figure 23: Mrs. Belmont's Louis XV paneled bedroom

Shortly after 10 p.m., one of our tour guides sought me out. A guest waiting for the ladies room had seen a woman, dressed in pink, sitting on the gilded sofa, a valuable museum piece located in front of the bedroom window. After she informed the guide that apparently someone had gone behind the rope, she looked back—and the lady in pink had disappeared.

"She didn't go past me, and she didn't go into the bathroom," she said.

Her description of the woman on the sofa—light blond hair, fair face, a pink gown—matched Ruth Tinney dressed in her pink burial gown.

Figure 24: Ruth Tinney in her pink gown, photo by Coit Studio

Chapter XVIII
Who Moved the Tools?

On New Year's Day, 1998, one of the seven furnaces required to heat the huge castle malfunctioned. That night the temperature outside was near zero. Normally, we would have noticed the cold, and from it discovered the inoperative furnace. But at 5 a.m., Donald took ill. We rushed him to the hospital, leaving no one in that section of the building.

A water pipe froze and split during the night. As the sun rose the next day, the pipe thawed and began gushing water. By the time the staff arrived at nine o'clock, water was pouring through the beautiful Haddon Hall-style ceiling in the library.

Figure 25: English Library.

Somebody located the shutoff valve and stopped the flow of water, but not before the entire room, with its bookshelves and rare carpet, was soaked. Despite our efforts to save it, a portion of the ornate ceiling collapsed onto the floor a few days later.

Months later, an eighty-year-old skilled artisan, called out of retirement, arrived to repair the damaged staff plaster work. Scaffolding had been erected for him throughout the room.

In his second week, after much of the surface preparation had been finished, he was hand-sculpting the molding, the most demanding part of his task. When he descended the scaffold to get a cup of coffee, he left his tools on the scaffold, as usual. When he returned this time, however, the tools were gone. He was distraught. He knew he hadn't misplaced them, not on that small platform where he had been working, so he assumed that someone had taken them. Donald and I were the only people in the house at the time, but we had not even entered the library that day. We were as perplexed as the man was. As we helped look for his tools, Don climbed the scaffold. Lo and behold, the tools were right where the man had been working. Only now, they were all neatly arranged.

The old man was dumbfounded by this, but we assured him that he had not been wrong about the disappearance of his tools. One of the Belcourt ghosts has been known to remove things and then replace them—sometimes minutes, sometimes days—later.

Over the years, many residents and guides at Belcourt have seen keys rise into the air above a table, float to the side, and then drop onto the floor. The Tinney family became accustomed to missing objects. We knew that, sooner or later, they somehow would reappear.

Chapter XIX
In Life I died, In Death I live

Donald Tinney had seen the ghosts of his mother and father, his Aunt Nellie, and his best friend, his cousin Frankie Betzer. Often he would describe them in detail, as if they were in the next room. The spirit of Belcourt Castle reflected Donald Tinney's declining health. He had planned to gift the castle to a university, one that would agree to continue the Tinney legacy. His collections would stay together. Staff and other friends of ours experienced a profound sadness as we were prepared to adjust to a retired life.

New Year's Eve of 2005 was the beginning of the Tinneys' 50th year at Belcourt Castle. Donald, who was generally uncomfortable in crowds and usually avoided social events, made a Herculean effort to participate in the festivities.

Figure 26: Harle and Donald Tinney at New Year's Eve black tie gala

Because of his arthritis pain, he did not like dancing, yet that night Donald and I danced five times and he danced with some of our dear friends to the nostalgic music of Larry Brown's Swing Lane Orchestra.

While we were sitting quietly one night shortly after New Year's, and several days afterward, he saw two girls in the living room. I could not see them. Donald continued to see his mother and father. He talked about Aunt Nellie, and he described the two girls in intimate detail. "One is a blonde. She's not so nice. One is a brunette. She's nice." I, who am usually loquacious, had no words. I saw nobody, yet I knew he was telling the truth about what he saw.

On January 16th, a bitter cold day, I had left Donald alone to attend a two-hour meeting. When my meeting was over, I could not find him. My co-worker and I searched for him throughout the house, and then outdoors, without success. The local police, state police, and the Coast Guard put every available officer into a search. For five hours, they braved freezing temperatures and pitch dark to no avail. My co-worker and his friends searched with flashlights near the water, calling for Donald until four in the morning.

Driving around the neighboring streets, I shivered and cried uncontrollably, though the car heater was blasting. "He is so cold," I kept repeating. All at once I felt warm and peaceful with the sensation that Donald was sitting beside me. His spirit communicated to me that he was at peace.

The next morning, Donald's best friend, the photographer Keith Henry, found his body in the water between two rocks. The blue jeans and gray sweater Donald was wearing matched the surroundings, even in daylight. It is likely that Don's soaring spirit guided Keith to the remains of his earthly shell. Donald Harold Tinney, 71, was dead.

All the things he had told me during the preceding months became clear. He had predicted his death. Even before we were married, he had rehearsed his epitaph: "In life I died, in death I live."

Once or twice in the past Donald had been near death. He described the experience like this:

"It was so beautiful. The music was indescribable. The gates were huge, but I could have designed them better." I laughed. Donald continued "I asked the figure, appearing just beyond the slightly open gate, if my father were there. I wanted to see Dad, but I understood it was not my time. I really did not choose to come back. It was so peaceful. The figure told me I must go back and that I would not remember any of this. But I do. The picture is in my mind. Maybe there was more that I don't remember. I do know that it is not far, it's just around the corner. Time is measured here on earth, but it's the opposite of time."

At Donald Tinney's funeral in Belcourt's Ballroom two of his friends saw him in the musician's balcony looking through the trefoils. It was typical of my husband to observe events from that private vantage point. His ghost has been seen several times in the organ loft on momentous occasions.

Figure 27: Organ loft in the French Gothic Ballroom

The ghost of Donald Tinney is a loving ghost. On the second month anniversary of his death, I had a dream. Donald came and put his arms around me as I slept. He was warm, gentle, and loving. There were no words, only thoughts. It was a perfect love, bestowing forgiveness for any hurt I had caused him, and delivering a silent message that he was sublimely happy and wanted me to come with him. But both of us knew, without saying it, that I have work to do; I am not ready. An important earthly task is just beginning. That same night, the 16th of March, 2006 Virginia Smith felt his presence as well. His message was one of love and comfort, perfect peace.

Chapter XX
Spirit Orb

Shortly after my husband's funeral I was looking at Larry Brown's photograph of Donald and me dancing on New Year's Eve and noticed a flaw in the photo. A round circle directly over Donald's head appeared to have a face like the man in the moon in it. I wondered if it might be an orb, a phenomenon well known and researched by scientifically educated ghost hunters. I had just read something in a magazine sent to me about spirit orbs.

The following day Belcourt received a phone call from Christopher Moon, the chief investigator for *Haunted Times* magazine. He was in town for the one day and desired an appointment. My appointments that day were in rapid succession, so I had no time to meet with him. He was persistent, and said they wanted "only a few minutes." My assistant, Shannon, offered to give them a tour, and I agreed to interrupt my schedule so that I could meet with them briefly.

Belcourt Castle turned out to be more intriguing to Chris Moon and his mom than they had expected, and they stayed for several hours. My meetings ended, and I was able to show them the photo Larry Brown had taken. They identified the circle in the picture as being a spirit orb. They also described the "vortex" in the photo, right where Donald's eyes seem to be focused, as the door between the worlds. This interpretation of the photograph bothered me. Was the open door to the other side calling to Donald?

Larry Brown was kind to provide a disc with his photos of New Year's Eve so I could enlarge the round object in the photo. That photo is a treasure.

Figure 28: Spirit orb over Donald Tinney's head on New Year's eve 2005. Photo by Larry Brown

Mr. Moon and his group returned to Belcourt in 2009 to conduct a witnessed investigation with meters. Their psychics are convinced that Donald Tinney is present in the ballroom. When his name was called there were blips on the meter. *Ghost Hunters*© also conducted a three-day investigation for the cable television SciFi Channel program. Their electronic equipment detected activity in areas which we did not anticipate.

The subject of ghosts is being accepted as a topic of conversation among people who would not have admitted to encountering such unexplained phenomena. Though the concept of ghosts is still controversial, there is much that we do not know. "Through a glass darkly," we observe the spirit world until we become a part of it, as we all will.

On these pages, I have recounted some, but by no means all, of my experiences with ghosts at Belcourt Castle. I have written about things I have seen myself, and I have repeated creditable stories told to me by others. Despite all that, I still tend to be skeptical, believing that many phenomena attributed to ghosts have logical explanations.

This book has been years in preparation, and as a result there are yet other stories to tell.

So is Belcourt haunted? I want to say "No!"

And yet ...

The Author

Harle Hope Hanson Tinney was born in Providence, RI, on April 15, 1941. Her father, Dr. Frederick Charles Hanson, was a prominent eye surgeon and her mother, Grace Hanson (née Williamson) was an accomplished violinist. Harle Hanson attended Classical High School and, upon graduating in 1959, attended Albion College in Michigan as a pre-medicine student with majors in chemistry and biology. She studied cello at Brown University and played in the Rhode Island Philharmonic Youth Orchestra while in high school and in the Albion Orchestra in college.

Figure 29: Harle Hope Hanson Tinney, Photo by Steven Stanley

In the summer of 1960, she became a tour guide at the Newport mansion Belcourt Castle, designed by Richard Morris Hunt and built as a summer residence for Oliver Belmont between 1891 and 1894. Since 1956, the Tinney family, Harold and Ruth Tinney, their son Donald, and Mrs. Tinney's aunt Nellie Fuller, had owned and operated the castle as a museum.

Harle married Donald Tinney in a formal ceremony on August 25, 1961, the first wedding at Belcourt. Within two weeks of moving into the castle, the new Mrs. Tinney had her first paranormal experience. She saw a full apparition of a monk who walked through a wall. Reluctant to share her experiences with her family at first, over the years such events were not uncommon. The hauntings at Belcourt Castle, which are believed to be attached mostly to the antiques in the collection, have been witnessed by residents, staff and visitors alike even to the present day.

Mrs. Tinney worked in the family stained glass studio from 1961 until 1989. Between 1966 and 1969, she and her family constructed Belcourt's famed Gold Coronation Coach, designed by her husband, Donald. A musician in her spare time, now, she may be found on the castle's third floor playing the 1864 pipe organ, a 26-rank tracker instrument built by E and G. G. Hook of Boston.

In 1972, she became a co-owner of Belcourt Castle. After 1984, as founder and CEO of two family catering companies, Mrs. Tinney became a wedding coordinator and managed in excess of twenty weddings and eighty events each year. She also served as secretary-treasurer of the non-profit body which governs the museum, the Royal Arts Foundation. In 1999, she became the foundation's executive director. Donald and Harle were knighted in the Sovereign Order of Orthodox Knights of St. John of Jerusalem, a charitable order with origins in Imperial Russia, in 1998.

Mrs. Tinney was widowed on Donald's sudden death on January 16, 2006. Since then she has managed Belcourt Castle, its collections (from thirty-three countries) and programs. She participates in Belcourt's ghost tours. She hosts special candlelight tours with a toast to world peace in honor of Belcourt's original owners, the Belmonts, a family of international diplomats, politicians and bankers since 1837.

In 2009, Mrs. Tinney allowed the acclaimed show "Ghost Hunters" to investigate Belcourt Castle in response to a new era of open-mindedness regarding the paranormal. She seeks to educate visitors on the history of hauntings and dispel any fear about the unknown. She plans to do more writing in 2010, marking her fiftieth year at Belcourt Castle.

The Author thanks family and friends who made contributions to this book:

The Board of Directors of the Royal Arts Foundation,
    Richard Zini, Jr., President
The Staff of Belcourt Castle
Donald Tinney
Tom Wingett
Keith A. Henry
Virginia Smith
William Rotunno
William Stroud
Michael Kathrens
Charles Hamm
Larry Brown, Sr.
Dr. Dorothie Maksym

LaVergne, TN USA
03 September 2010
195655LV00016B/5/P